I0212586

Dialogues Among Lost Tourists

poems by

Tony Magistrale

Finishing Line Press
Georgetown, Kentucky

Dialogues Among Lost Tourists

Publisher: Leah Maines

Editor: Christen Kincaid

Cover Art: *Gondola Park* by Michael J. Strauss.
          Visit his website at: www.mjstrauss.com

Author Photo: Kathy FitzGerald

Cover Design: Elizabeth Maines McCleavy

Printed in the USA on acid-free paper.
Order online: www.finishinglinepress.com
          also available on amazon.com

Author inquiries and mail orders:
Finishing Line Press
P. O. Box 1626
Georgetown, Kentucky 40324
U. S. A.

Table of Contents

Part One: The Lost Fathers

Part Two: Dialogues Among Lost Tourists

Part Three: Dialogues in Paints and Marbles

Excellent friends and colleagues read and critiqued many early drafts of these poems, and this book is dedicated to all of them: Michael Strauss, Alexis Fancher, David Huddle, Philip Baruth, Jim DeFilippi, Larry Bennett, Ken Wagner, Sarah E. Turner, Colleen Dolan, Norman Tederous, Hubert Zapf, Klaus Post and Major Jackson. I love and am grateful for each of you.

Part One: The Lost Fathers

Photograph of My Father

"I should set up some sort of shrine for these Bouquets of time."
—Baron Wormser

He's naked, except for swimming trunks.
Standing in a foot of warm ocean.
Because it is a b&w image,
The water is the same blank color of the sky.
It looks like a perfect beach day.
I have no idea where he is—
Mexico on vacation?
Guam at the end of the war?
Adrift on the Pacific rim?
Anyway, he's far away from the snows of Buffalo.
But not as far as he is now.
His bald head & compact body remind me of Picasso.
He's beatific, positively beaming with energy.
I never remember him happier than he is in this photograph.
His hands are raised in supplication towards the sun.
He's reaching out to embrace the future,
Although his future is now past.
He's young. Completely on his own.
He hasn't learned how to suffer yet.
That will come later.

Memory Not Found Inside Our Family Album

Not much older than twelve
      a new state adventure for me
            our family's first overnight trip anywhere

winding through patchwork hills and valleys
      late autumn to Pennsylvania State University
            in search of a Hail Mary cure for my sister's worsening

cerebral palsy. There are photographs of her walking,
      standing upright, my father directly behind, her fingers
            entwined in his, their arms outstretched together—

a dual crucifixion. A week's worth of white-coated,
      doctor-specialists probing and wondering, *Did she ever*
            crawl? Describe her birthing experience. Their science

and advanced degrees as efficacious as my mother's
      nightly rain of prayers shed upon the blank beads of a rosary
            in arresting my sister's wretched descent, her body's

wracking seizures and escalating war
      against itself. In another year, she couldn't get
            off the couch to use the bathroom. Adult diapers

a permanent part of my mother's wash load.

Family Man

Walking across Delaware Avenue to the Statler Hotel
for a meeting or to sign important papers
(how important are any of them now?)
pulling his coat together with one hand,
holding on to his black fedora with the other,
headlong into Lake Erie white wind
as specks of ice fling themselves between office buildings,
another interminable winter of slush
and burnt snow, Buffalo skies the ashen gray of death.

Each Christmas Eve I would meet him
downtown. We would drink expensive red wine
until December darkness drove us out into it
and talk turned sentimental.
Toughest trial lawyer I ever saw work a courtroom
had to wipe away tears
whenever he heard the song *White Christmas.*

For forty years a compliant prisoner
in his own home. Work his addiction and escape,
his only refuge against the daily humiliations,
the tedious boredom, the inane dinner chatter.
He used to tell me *someone is going*
to have to die first before anything can change.
And I wondered where was that trial lawyer
in the face of such protracted misery?

Back then, a man just didn't disappear,
up and leave his family on their own.
He tried to explain this to me every time
I would ask, but that was before I understood
anything about being a family man.

Entropy

Every second five million cells divide inside us—
copying their DNA like an overheated Xerox machine.
My father used to say the human body is a mechanism
too complex for its own good; built magnificently,
but not to last.
Entropy x cell mitosis x years on the planet = cancer,
the ultimate extension of Murphy's Law.

When it came for him
lurking within the shadows of his own body,
it erupted in the forested nodules of his left lung,
metastasized to his spine, where the elevator
took it up to his brain, top floor, penthouse suite,
everybody out.

As a kid, my father taught me the sport of racquetball,
lobbing the small blue sphere softly
against the front wall, offering my first lesson
in geometry. *Angles, the game's*
all about playing the right angles.
A mathematical consistency that entropy undercuts,
like those moments when the ball
ricochets off a crack in the floor
or a corner joint and breaks cruelly, unexpectedly,
thwarting every law of geometry
as it did the last time we played together,
lobbing the ball softly back to my father
whose frail body stood alone in the left corner,
both of us aware but not saying
he could no longer divine the right angles.

Vegas

The last year that he lived
I told my father I wished to take him on a trip

Anywhere in the world he wanted to go,
One last family vacation reduced

To what was left of our family.
Of all places—he picked Vegas.

Perhaps the city reminded him of better days
When he was young and cancer-less;

I think he longed for one more chance
To roll the dice wantonly,

Put a stack of chips on black seven,
Do the math necessary to hit

Twenty-one. Maybe he just wanted to glimpse again
A pretty girl dressed as a chandelier.

The lights and sounds of Vegas
Were meant to provide a distraction,

The opportunity for both of us
To laugh as we used to laugh, without deliberation.

But each night he was asleep by eight o'clock
Leaving me to wander up and down

The concrete length of The Strip
In search for something not for sale.

My Father's Shoes

He had been dying for two full days
before we arrived in Buffalo,
his young grandsons and me,
and when I told him I needed to feed
his children some dinner, a Friday night
fish fry, promising we'd come
right back
to spend the rest of the evening
with him in the darkened hospice room
that smelled of antiseptic and clean linen,
he looked up at me and said,
without rancor or sadness,
Get my shoes. I'm going, too.
He wouldn't be requiring shoes
where he was going, but I was
the only one in the room
who grasped this certainty
and I despised the knowing.

Anniversary

Thirteen years ago tonight
I walked into that awful room, the Cheyne-Stokes
race that had been running inside his chest
finally at rest. I was not alone,
my uncle told me to anoint his hands and face,
already hard cold and white as alabaster,
with holy water, then kiss my father
good-bye. I remember
the soft buzz of the single florescent light
above us. We said little else,
what was there left to say
when all the energy had left this room hours ago?
I wish I had stayed with his body a little longer,
but there didn't seem to be much point
since that body was no longer his home. And
my own sons were alone
back at his house asleep in his king-sized bed;
they were waiting for their father,
and would be needing breakfast
soon.

The Brisbane Building

3500 miles away, my friend Larry
E-mails me pictures he has taken
of the Brisbane Building in downtown

Buffalo, the office where my father worked
for forty years. Its sandy brown edifice
looks unchanged in the twenty years since

he left as a tenant, when Larry's
exterior photographs push me back
inside and the past comes floating down to me,

standing there, curbside next to Larry,
looking up, remembering vaguely
the people we are no longer, having left them

inside that building. The legacy
we are gifted and what we leave behind
are only glancing images, slips of memories,

like the blinding fractured suns
that glint white haloes off rows of windows
in Larry's photographs, as I struggle

to find my father's receding face,
his hand waving behind a thick glass window
from his office up on the fourth floor

following silently as I turn away from him
and the Brisbane Building making my way
towards the bus station to go back to school.

Tony Soprano Sleeps with the Fishes

"What're ya gonna do?"
—Anthony John Soprano

He always knew he was destined
to become *capofamiglia*, a Captain of Industry,
following his old man and Uncle Junior.
Tony did them one better: carved out
a palace in the Jersey suburbs
with not one, but two *principesse*.

And while he never finished college
or learned the right lessons from the History channel
and those gangster movies he watched on DVD,
Dr. Melfi knew his panic attacks were about more
than rare *capocollo* or a misplaced family of ducks.

He was a man of capacious appetites—
loved sports and women and food,
but most of all, he loved money.
Maybe we loved him because Soprano was no better
or worse than either you or me;
if you live long enough in this world
nobody comes out clean.

Thousands mourned in church when he died,
not from a bullet but an overburdened heart,
his coffin surrounded by grieving family
and made-men from all the families,
and none of them was a bit surprised
when Meadow cried the loudest.

Dracula in Crisis

He recognizes his arrogant bravado
as a mechanism of self-defense;
he's been spending way too much time by himself.
Even those obnoxious Jehovah's Witnesses
haven't knocked on his castle door in decades.
The ancient coins bulging his pockets
won't work in any vending machine.

It's mostly an inconvenience until it turns
personal. He can feel his estrangement growing
among these pasty-faced rubes, and not just
his coworkers at the blood bank. He spies
disgruntled villagers sharpening wood, how they
no longer bother to hide making the sign of the cross
whenever his black Cadillac glides by.
The local teenagers toilet paper
his wrought iron fence every Saturday night,
and now the cops are hassling him
about wolf shit all over the neighborhood.

He knows it's probably time to pack up his coffins
and move to Pennsylvania, unearth some new girls
who find his old world *ennui* and pick-up lines
charming instead of creepy, but he's reluctant to leave—
where is he likely to find another dentist
who can keep his mouth shut anywhere else?

Language Matters

The spectacle of raising teenage boys
Nothing like the veiled mysteries of teenage girls,
Its opposite entirely. His mother's
Adamant refusal midway through junior year
To step inside that school again, leaving me
To parent alone a conference in Mr. Burke's office
For inappropriate language usage in Health class:
Does anyone know the origins of the AIDS
Epidemic? The teacher's wary decision to call
On such a confident hand: *Fucking Monkeys.*
Not wrong! I argued in filial support. Nevertheless,
Three days suspension, whether *fucking*
Is employed as an adjective or a verb.

Fathers and Daughters

She's the girlfriend his wife
has permitted him to keep—for years she nests
in the same familiar spot on his lap
smelling like the inside of a candy shop,
testing the full repertoire of her emerging powers:
fluttery kisses to his face, the new sundress
that requires his approval, earnest questions
his wife knew all the answers to long ago.

Then, one day without warning
she stops visiting that lap and starts hanging
with a guy her father knows is a serial killer.
Each night he wakens to the scent of chloroform
hidden under the seat in a van without windows,
reeking of sex and pot. Dad would love nothing more
than to punch out the lights of this hairy interloper,
but it's all he can do
to manage a chronic-level depression
and his wife's condescending grin.

What Mr. Richel Knew

When the big yellow school bus finally
disgorged us after a day of conjugating

irregular Latin verbs and algebraic integers
destined to swallow me whole,

I would walk Carol Richel home
and imagine her father's red face

glaring out every window of his white suburban
split-level. He knew I had been admiring

a ribbed suture running the long length
of Carol's left black stocking the entire ride.

He could see teenage testosterone
oozing out, staining my shirt a bright red C.

At night, he knew I leaned out
my window in defiance of physics,

telescoping around the blank block
of Maplemere Elementary and into Carol's

pink bedroom, where I watched her model
Victoria's Secret bras and panties, practice

tongue kissing in front of her mirror.
The only thing Carol's father never knew

was the summer night his daughter drank
half a bottle of peppermint Schnapps

and collapsed, face-down unconscious,
shoehorned in my stunned lap. I didn't dare move

an inch, never touched a hair on Carol's perfect
yellow head, even after peppermint-scented

vomit seared the crotch Mr. Richel knew
would someday spawn the seed of Satan.

Part Two: Dialogues Among Lost Tourists

Dialogues Among Lost Tourists

After their disastrous weekend in D.C.,
when she chose to sleep in her pantyhose
to reinforce unequivocally her determination

to impress upon him the certainty
that it was over between them, he watched
her walk away from the crowded Amtrak station

and just before she slid back
into the driver's seat of her little blue Honda,
flashing him one final extended glimpse

of painfully exquisite calf and thigh,
he saw her pause in the parking lot
to answer a question from some lost tourist,

turn around and point her left index finger
with its blood-red half-moon nail
directly at him and it was then he realized

the world was larger than this station
and his sorrow, and this was only
her way of providing directions.

In the Airport

Buttoned-up businessmen in perpetual transit
pace the length of tiled corridors under florescent
white light, arms gesticulating wildly
like overweight birds in frustrated flight,
seconds before my realization
these men are attached to Bluetooth devices
nestled in their ears—images of madness
preclude orders from Poughkeepsie, desperate entreaties

home. In a corner chair
a woman reading a vampire novel
tucks one booted calf under the other
so that her black skirt rises
exposing just enough thigh
to remind us that sex
can erupt anytime, anywhere,

even here, where the public intercom
dispenses periodic recorded warnings
that all bags are subject to random acts
of obliteration. Outside,
just beyond double-plated safety glass,
ectoplasmic plumes of Jet-A exhaust
bloom in the serene spring morning
awaiting our restless urge.

Before This Was My Book

Purchased at a local yard sale
for two dollars, it belonged to someone
else, a young woman I would surmise

who left small feminine pencil notes in the margins
and underscored lines from her favorite poems
meant to be read by a man she loved

but felt compelled to leave. There's no
explanation for why their love had to be aborted,
only images already receding into memory—

I will remember the morning light . . .
Getting dressed for you before our meeting . . .
The smell of sex, your fingers entwined in my hair . . .

How can I ever hope to make this book
my own after she has evoked language
so intimate to these two alone?

Perhaps I need rather to adopt
the more cynical attitude of her lover,
who must certainly have understood

the importance of these words from his mistress,
yet ended up abandoning them anyway—
which is I suppose the fate of most books

and many love affairs—gleefully
opened, explored—and then discarded
to await the fresh caress of some stranger's hands.

A Short Treatise on Time

"There are days when the fear of death illuminates everything."
—Ted Kooser

I'm weary of bemoaning so many lost
days,

as if we ever had any choice other than the one-way
ticket with a time-stamp securely in place,

like those issued for certain train journeys
in Europe: use it by Sunday afternoon

or forfeit the ride. Or when you buy a quart of milk
and it sits souring on its ass in your refrigerator
because you forgot it, off doing other things

instead of eating breakfast. Of course it's an unfair deal
and you would have hired a high-priced lawyer
to negotiate the fine print,

but the gods never consulted you
before forwarding your contractual obligations.

Now that death has switched places
from the distant dot at the horizon
creeping up in the rear-view mirror

to hovering around the face you shave
every morning, you find yourself often
stranded on the *autobahn* of memory,

drunk on nostalgia's exit ramp,
which is not a good place to linger very long;

beware of any drug that promotes forgetfulness
paving over potholes from the past.

Try remembering this instead: you didn't understand
much less appreciate

half of what you did with your youth;
and you certainly wouldn't have bothered

to watch rain fill the still surfaces of a dark pond
with dozens of perfect circles.

Westchester Pastoral

The bright true-colored suburbs of white
middle-aged marrieds residing in expansive houses
where a light is always lit,
their children off at boarding school or
under the vigilant eye of the Swedish *au pair.*
Such duplicitous comfort in those first paragraphs
as they linger on corners of gauzy summer twilights—
always a weekend, women in floral party dresses
and high heels, Sunday poolside hangovers, sprinklers clicking
a fine mist syncopation across a republic of green,
the thick scent of barbequed flesh
drifting from some backyard a block away.

Westchester pastoral,
an envelope where a sheaf of American time
folds neatly inside, like old love letters secreted in an attic.
A housewife, not a little drunk, distracted
by her own reflection in a hallway mirror,
discerns a college girl ghost with long blond hair
and muses *every day brings another little funeral.*
Her husband bears the weight of his masculinity
like a second mortgage; at night he lifts off their bed
remembering the distant conquests of women
whose faces are now impossible for him to detail.

On a street named Shady Hill Lane,
among the tangled roots of broken promises
in the troubled undergrowth,
a little man wearing his hair cropped short
impeccably dressed in bow tie and suit coat
points to some roses in his neighbor's front yard
and notes the petals dropping off one
by one.

Paint It Black

Stuck in the commute atop her Ducati
she's inconvenienced by a long traffic light,
sleek line of shiny black leather curves—
gloves, high boots, tight jeans, bomber jacket—
welded like sex to the machine.
She's been rehearsing this fashion utterance
in front of a hallway mirror all winter long.
When I pull up alongside atop my Schwinn,
she can't hear what I'm asking,
exits her Darth Vader helmet
releasing an explosion of honey-blond hair.
Good morning, Mademoiselle Licorice. First one to the next light
buys the supersized can of ArmorAll?
She shoots back an imperious look,
the kind my mother saved for church,
excommunicates me in a plume of fluorocarbons
and noisy black blur.

The Essence of Cool

He slouches against his motorcycle,
ripped muscle shirt and tight jeans,
the essence of cool,
might agree he shares something
in common with Brando and Dean
if only he understood what that means.
He hasn't expended much energy
studying old movies or going to school;
he's been busy refining
the essence of cool.
The neighbors shake their heads and wonder
when he's likely to get on track,
make a commitment to some woman
who will make him come back
before the bars all close down,
find a job, settle down.
The honest ones secretly envy him, too,
his complete lack of tact,
his ability to travel anywhere
with his possessions in one sack.
Perhaps someday he'll join them—
buy a place of his own, take medicine
for ulcers, bed by ten, kids to bemoan.
But tonight he's a shadow,
more dream than a fact,
happy child wearing the body of a man
without regrets or urge to look back.

Teachable Moment

That first glorious
convertible-worthy, top-down day
my buddy and I pull up
alongside a yellow bus
packed with high school students
on their journey home. At a red light
everyone inside
rushes to our side of the bus,
mud-streaked half windows descend, comments fly:
Way cool car, Dudes. You guys are awesome,
can we get a ride? I catch the eye of one kid
sitting alone
in the back next to a window. He's
the only one not glad to make our acquaintance,
wrinkling his face in a grimace of displeasure.
Before the light changes,
my buddy offers some ancient advice: *Stay in school;*
you'll be cruising in your own car with the top down.
The kid in the back
sticks up his middle finger
to remind us
high school's always a prison
especially on fine spring afternoons.

High School Reunion

Forty years separate us like a wedge of ocean,
a chasm so broad and deep
the other side, the starting point we trusted
would connect us forever, has become a dim glow
at the horizon. We telescope ourselves back,
struggle to recover lost ground, like birds
that have flown a great distance trying to recall
the topography of their trip. This is, after all,
why we are gathered here—to take some refuge
from a past long gone and for whom
only the people in this room remain
to reconfigure it. How beautiful we were then,
wearing our innocence like a tight pair of jeans,
certain of only one thing—that we were never
going to die—and ready to get on the future
like it was a streetcar in a strange, new town:
Oh, take us anywhere but here,
and now, here is where we have migrated,
this hotel ballroom with its fusty smell,
standing with cold drinks in in our hands
swapping tales of children and grandchildren,
the lesions of divorce and addiction,
multiple jobs and forced relocations,
recognizing distant friends by their eyes
as the last unadulterated body part, and slightly
stunned by the discovery that our truest connection
turns out to be parallel narratives of survival.
But it was when I overheard my former
high school girlfriend
remark to another classmate,
I got exactly what I wanted,
that filled me with sudden mystery, her words
left wondering in my ears,
was this more curse than gift?

She

For Alexis Fancher

Would catwalk into school bake sales
and boys' varsity basketball games
sutured into black leather miniskirts
and leopard-spotted jumpsuits with matching
stiletto pumps. That winter,
she raised the temperature of every
high school gymnasium in the state.

She wondered why the neighborhood wives
failed to include her when they went out for coffee,
why their husbands wanted her kid
to play on their baseball team each spring.

Alongside her assorted cannoli,
the other mothers' frosted cupcakes tasted
frumpy. With no effort, she commanded
bolts of brazen energy from her bedroom
to rumble down the streets of Fairyland—
in vain did diligent mothers labor
to avert the eyes of their daughters
already committed to finding
that exact color red at the mall.

Bad Girl

That was what she called herself
Every time I went to visit her
Down in her mother's basement
Nothing but a mattress on the floor
Two chairs and a television set
I would enter through the back door
After I dropped the cheerleaders home
By curfew at their fathers' front doors
She was always there watching Carson
Wearing only bra and panties
Because she never had to work in the morning
Smoking cigarettes or painting her nails
When I was seventeen
As much eroticized as terrified
By her fleshy strangeness
Her red lips and hair
A vampire-like Lucy Westenra
After *The Change* to voluptuousness
As I sat on the straight-back chair
Across from her bed
Uttering banalities that made her snort smoke
Holding onto my virginity like a crucifix
Uncertain how to let it go

Graduation

I'd just opened a window
to let in another glorious May day
midway through a conversation
with Anthony Clifton about how many more

credits would be required for him to graduate
next May, when Kiera Tambara interrupted,
minutes after a shower, her chestnut hair
still a damp tango, wearing a tight purple

sundress without any straps that announced
she was already halfway to a summer tan.
She handed me her take-home final,
sighed, *that's the last paper or examination*

I will ever write for the rest of my life,
twirled a blithe 180, and vanished from sight
leaving my office smelling like a candy shop.
Anthony continued to plod the road

towards graduation, when I suggested
We ought to give pause. When a spring tornado
descends on Kansas or Oklahoma
what do you think the people in those places say

once they realize it has gone away
leaving them alive another day?
Mr. Clifton lifted his worried head,
Perhaps I should take out another loan?

Ode to a New Pair of Louboutin Boots

Savor their soft buttery weightlessness
to enchant even the most discerning fetishist,
their spanking out-of-the-box animal scent.
Gleaming jet-black stockings bearing invisible zippers
adhere the length of skyscraper legs to seal in size sevens.
Then, as an almost startling afterthought,
the fierce firings of both stilettos,
walking the length of a pencil thin tightrope—
strobes of perpendicular scissors
challenge the shine of puddles in a rain-filled night,
each step a resounding crack cherry-red syncopation
turning heads on anonymous sidewalks,
blood boot prints atop fresh snow
rising from beneath a sea of black,
double homicides that refuse to look back.
Straddling the line between
tres chic and dominatrix,
contrasting mixtures of hard & soft, like enameled nails
emerging from inside the night of a glove.

What's Anonymous About It?

Periodically, we have this same conversation,
old wine poured into new bottles,
how hard it is to stay sober
in a culture that is always
uncorking, popping open, decanting & unscrewing
to escape from being so bottled-up.
Isn't that just like America
to hawk the imbibe with snappy ballads & tipsy commercials
where everyone is bubbly & irresistible,
making the trip to blackout so damn sexy,
& then punish its indulgence with impunity,
like being held accountable for every tremor
your brain ferments at night
& insists you swallow in one great gulp.

In Costco's Parking Lot

Amidst the hundreds of asphalt spaces
open-ended rectangles defined by clean white lines,
two dozen black & white SUVs
each containing a woman—wives & mothers,
homemakers all—the drone of their powerful engines
humming against the soft serenity of a Wednesday morning,
each staring out blankly at one another
from behind tinted safety glass, windows up,
engulfed in the cool pulse of air conditioning,
strands of recently frosted hair fluttering softly
as waves of radiant heat shimmer up from car hoods,
awaiting the imminent arrival of scruffy worker men
who bend to raise thick gray metal gates
that will provide access to rows of plentitude,
silver carts filled to their meniscus,
the SUVs packed with plastic rainbows of bottles & boxes
& reams of white toilet paper
until there is only room enough for each woman
sitting alone among the vast amplitude of America
to drive herself home.

Recent Death in the Back of a Pickup Truck

Barely visible beneath his brown flanks
And snow-white down underside,
A long thin gash of vermilion, not red
So much as purple. The royal color

And the slit exposing his gutted entrails
Surprised me: I did not expect such raw brilliance,
Especially against the muddy camouflage
Of a body that had shielded him well

For so many years. His eyes, wide open
But already gone dim, a hazy gray
Film, like cataracts, filling nearly both
Sockets, made me wonder with what shock

The bullet must have entered—
Time only to exhale and collapse
A warm heap upon wet leaves
Of forest spotted with patches of snow,

One last look around at fading autumn,
At his crippled self, at the single black branch
That held the half-eaten berries or apple
Left hovering directly above.

Summer Nights

"Ain't no doubt about it / we were doubly blessed"
—Meatloaf

Forty years ago when we resembled
more our children
than our parents
I would pick you up
at your mother's front door
or the 7-11 store
where you worked the register
and we would drink
to rehydrate and forget the day
until the rest of the world
went home to bed
leaving us the alien morning
among black silhouettes of bulbous houses
the fog-haloed street lights
suburban lawns turned silver
sopped with morning dew
kissing and pushing
against one another
because we were young
residing in an envelope
that included the night sounds
swoosh of traffic miles away
a soothing wet melody
as you bore down
in the front seat of my father's car
whispering *don't talk just breathe me in*
and I did drinking
what was left of your fading perfume
hiding beneath the workday's perspiration
entangled in your hair's long curtain
somehow even then aware
that these were no mere
summer nights
like the dawn itself
the future held off at the horizon

still unborn
where it couldn't find us
or change us
until it did

Summer Sunday Love Song

They drive down the drowsy highway,
he in front, steering the small motor scooter.
She rides behind him in a bikini and sunglasses,
her tanned arms around his bare chest;
neither wears a helmet, their hair streaming
like two unfurled banners in the breeze.
Those of us stuck growing old
inside air-conditioned cars and minivans
glance at them as tourists, but only for a moment,
then they are gone—a dark fragment
receding in our rear-view mirrors.
I hope they both remember
their short ride together this afternoon
with some of the reverence that it held for me,
their simple trip to the grocery store
then back to her parents' house for a late supper.

Seven Hours to Munich

In the aisle seat adjacent to yours
snores a girl whose ample bottom has enveloped the mutually

shared armrest border,
            spilling over into your already highly circumscribed space.

For seven hours you say good-bye to comfort,
breathe in the exhausted air of others
            so thoroughly recycled

it tastes like tin. Seven hours of cottonmouth,
of waiting in line to use the dollhouse bathroom
while the Duty Free cart of discounted booze and cigarettes
            presses its intrusive edge

into your back, squeezing you up against the door
that separates the drowsy guts of this machine
from thirty-six thousand feet of dark uncharted
            nothingness.

Then, as if by magic, deposited back on earth,
you are transported into the glorious hospitality of a hot shower,
a glass of wine in your hand, the sound
of gently cascading water somewhere
            out of sight. The late winter afternoon, gray and friendless,

seeps into your room, but under the shield of this down comforter
in a benevolent bed with plenty of space to luxuriate,
            your body finally drops

down—deeper into the folds of freshly-ironed
sheets, crisp and cool to your nakedness.

Large flakes of wet snow erupt outside,
snap against the window and
            disappear, like the woman

who sat in the seat next to you for seven hours
and never said a word.

Sunday Morning in Munich

Millions asleep in their beds or busy preparing eggs and breads
or exercising on bicycles and treadmills,
while I stand nearly alone in this darkened museum
transfixed by ancient black and white news footage of the Reich,
steel helmeted heads marching in symmetrical human blocks
down the same streets I have just recently walked,
festooned with long swastika banners dripping
like lines of blood down the impassive faces of gray buildings.
And suddenly there he is
entering the screen to the right
in his arrogant display, his neatly pressed suit and combed hair,
the object of the crowd's narcotic trance,
love-struck assembly of pretty Deutschen blonds
and their misinformed children. In another,
he greets the grieving widows of soldiers
recently massacred at the Eastern front.
One of the women standing in line can't stop
sobbing, and so he pauses in front of her for more than
the perfunctory handshake distributed to the others
and cups his cold dry hand, the same hand
he uses to salute the troops he sends off into carnage,
along the side of her fractured face. Although the woman
remains inconsolable, the unexpected gesture is what
freezes me, and I must view the scene again,
and yet again: Is this a moment of compassion?
Those eyes, unsmiling and iron black in their midnight graininess,
do they soften? Can the greatest prick in history
be moved by the tears of this bereft woman?
But then the newsreel shifts to a fresh montage
and he is once again goose-stepping in time
on ancient cobblestones alongside an entourage of thousands
to the silent music of the dead.

The Gift

I once saw a long black limousine
Rumble down a cobblestone street at dusk
In the backseat window a blonde bride
Her pretty face open to the world,
Lipsticked smile, like a big red bow,
Greeting everyone she passed on the streets
And along the sidewalks—a wordless bond
Instantly forged in our universal recognition
That pure joy deserves its place in this world, too.

It hardly matters where this bride
Was headed—to or from the church,
Or even if her marriage turned out happily.
What endures is the wedding gift
She kindly bestowed—a small intimacy
Entrusted to total strangers
And that, years later, I swear,
Each time I walk by that same street
Still arouses in me envy for her bridegroom.

Venetian Notes

Like Venus, pulled from beneath the sea
and suspended, otherworldly, stiletto scaffolding
in muck and detritus. What roots here
flourishes here. But nowhere else.
No transplants into salt water soil.

The railway station is more than
la fermata terminale, literal end of the line.
That first glimpse of water and sky to flat horizon
amidst the silence of machines,
the noisy need-to-be-somewhere-else.
Venetian time, which is
static and fluid simultaneously, indulgently surreal,
asserts its dreamlike trance.

Venice was once:
Bank of Europe. Capital of Europe.
Museum of Europe. Brothel of Europe.

After the cock and ball statuary of Rome,
this city takes a decidedly feminine curve
in the Grand Canal's serpentine sweep to San Marco,
in subterranean stillness, fallopian tube
labyrinths, the sugary beauty of glass and lace.
Everything in Venice reflects itself—
feminine narcissism inside shop displays,
water mirrors, even puddles of rain.
Two young women on their way to work
stand in front of rectangular store window
patting gloved fingers against dank hair,
checking the curve of their lipsticks in glass.

Jumble of cul-de-sacs and surprise piazza unfolding
small spaces give birth to large spaces—
and then shrink and bend into sequestered
calli, worn gray stones moist

from sea and sky. Entangled alleyways
and short, high-humped bridges, stilled canals
containing putrid green waters.

Boats of all sizes and shapes
chug loudly along the Grand Canal,
cacophonous music of the sea; here,
rush-hour traffic floats instead of rolls,
sliding and sluicing, exhaling thick violet plumes
of exhaust, metal hulls
rising and falling, hypnotically slap and bump
heaving breathlessly across lagoon's watery plain.

What must it be like to be a full-time
citizen of Venice, to recognize this same
full moon, *la luna cacciatore,*
reflected in the canalazzo at midnight
and on the vast body of the Adriatic,
deep enough to accommodate obese cruise ships
squeezing through the Grand Canal, its glimmering
light refracted into yellow filaments
absorbed by, shimmering off
undulating sea waves, a 1400 year-old
moon viewed by Casanova's love-struck
mistresses and Tintoretto's sole illumination
from which his wraithlike shapes were born.

The color black slips into Venice—mold on white marble
facades, the water at a distance or after sunset—
moonlight fractured in breaking waves rising on a breeze
lacing a canal.

More than anywhere else, this city belongs
to history, a museum of itself
weighed down by a past that always wants
to drown present and future—dank pools of musty odors,
reminiscent of the grave.

My first time in Venice I was twenty-one.
Ken Wagner and I wandering nowhere in particular,
as if pulled by moon and tides to the sea,
when we stumbled accidentally into San Marco's square,
giant piazza ours alone, its magnificent silence,
a cool wind swirling newspapers and dead flowers
in circles around our feet; above our heads,
the *campanaria* measured the solemn hours to dawn.

Near the end of *Don't Look Now,*
a film where Venice is the main character,
Donald Sutherland looks out over sun-dappled
emerald waves to see his wife, a supple
Julie Christie, dressed in funereal clothes
and riding implacably at the helm of a black *traghetta.*
His effort to contact her across the busy canal
nets only silence, for the vision he sees is not real,
but another Venetian fabrication of time and sight,
his mind residing on ground as unstable as the mud of the Adriatic,
swept up and pursued by malign design
that carries out its terrible work inside Venetian shadows.

Ancient, glass and water avatar, perpetual carnival town,
reclaimed island of dark loneliness, Edgar
Poe's dead city of the sea, haunted by ghosts
from a thousand different epochs,
sinking into the east.

Milan

Because she sent out so many mixed messages, it's remarkable how deeply she affected me. Tourists, those who choose not to avoid her completely, heading east to Venice or south to Florence, even natives who labor in her shops and office buildings, call her a dirty whore, and to her face; an old bitch gone in the teeth, as Pound said a century ago. And like a whore, they appreciate her value only in terms of generating money—but that's their loss, even as they abandon her each night and every weekend for places more refined: north to Switzerland or the quaint little condo in the suburbs. Scary and sometimes mean, she takes a cruel pleasure out of intimidating the naïve and unworldly, those lacking a thirst for adventure; if safety and comfort remain your primary considerations, you would best explore somewhere else. I came to Milan when I was 29, and susceptibly innocent. All my life I'd lived in Disney World. Milan was a final rite of passage into adulthood. Not knowing any better, I'd subsisted on an exclusive diet of compliant cheerleaders and pretty country rubes wearing pastel skirts. Milan was the first woman to show up for a date who was smarter and savvier than me, smoldering under heavy makeup, a tight leather skirt and killer heels, chain-smoking her way through a multilingual dinner, and then pulling me into dark alleys for drunken French kissing. I hated her for a long time before I realized I was in love with her—vampiric and unapologetic, she could punish with impunity—as in the used clusters of bloodied heroin needles I would find discarded every morning curbside outside my apartment building. But because I stuck around long enough, she taught me things I never would have learned some place else: that glamour often lurks beneath a black veil of dust—and while you may be young only once, the memory of a beautiful woman, and the city where she resides, refuses to age.

Vermont Hillsides

You'll look back and remember this
As one of late September's last gifts
When its soft afternoon light
Resembled most a caress
Along the assembled faces of a thousand trees
Holding their breaths, standing erect
Black and tan—the leaves of birch and beech
On the edge of death
Stirring ever so slightly
As if tickled by unseen fingers—
Nothing moving for miles
Except that pale, vanilla light
Shying away so gracefully,
Retreating into western corner
Behind a landscape of shadows
That gives way, reluctantly, to night.

Winter Air

How sweet this winter air
so soft and light, puts big dogs
to sleep as they nestle in beside
firelight that licks the roof of a blackened hearth,
while outside twilight beckons—distant
orange glow at the southern edge of the lake
cold and clear—it will be 20 below
tonight.

       So many winter days accumulating
like snow on the ground, and how many
resemble this one, a childhood in Buffalo,
career in Vermont: a lifetime of shoveling it
beneath stars brighter than any summer night,
Orion's red Betelgeuse shines alongside Castor and Capella,
as small white ghosts billow out from my lungs
in silver-plumed exoskeletons.

How quickly these winter days dissemble,
pass into one another, each afternoon
moving across an abbreviated sky—
when suddenly the faint scent of evergreen
on the air, an early Christmas morning,
my parents' house silent and still as a spirit,
a hand on the stair banister
descends from beneath a child's distant sleep.

Early April Afternoon

The first one where you can sit
outside in a lawn chair in the sun.
Too cold to linger for very long
the wind marches back from March
whipping through the tops of pines
reminding the dog & me
of winter still hovering all around
in yellow grass & brown leaves.
But the dog would have me
scratch that spot
behind her ears
a few moments
longer
in the pure translucent light
that pours down
over us
sent from the future.

Summer's Cusp

At 8:30 p.m. on the last day of May
nature's aria rising into the suburban soundtrack
from out of marshlands and woods
the escalating *burrrape* of invisible insects and aquatic amphibians
opening their throats, pulsating their wings,
in rehearsal for the dramatic nocturne
that fills the soft evening air in a steady chorus
celebrating life, or is it death, probably both,
as bedroom and tomb are juxtaposed for every species—
the cyclic throb containing as much horror
as hope, as much collective scream
as rhythmic heartbeat.

Part Three: Dialogues in Paints and Marbles

Dialogues

After hours of wandering room to room,
legs bear the weight of too many eras,
head filled with so much human emotion—
transfixed by variances of spring light in Provence,
mythological allegories, crucified Christs,
burning war ships and parliaments,
and enough naked female breasts
to eroticize an entire strip club.

I contain so much color I must have eaten a Jackson Pollock.

A class of young schoolchildren
instructed by their perky teacher:
Look carefully at the painting.
What do you see?
What do you feel?

In the French Impressionist room,
I turn to the lone woman standing next to me.
We are strangers brought together
in front of a particularly purple panel
of *Water Lilies,* commissioned late in the painter's life
when Monet was nearly blind.

I want to ask her:
What do you see?
What do you feel?
But we turn away from one another at the same time,
exit the room in opposite directions,
she towards an exhibit of medieval religious art
while I enter the American Realism wing.

We might as well exist in different epochs,
separated by centuries.

When the Guard Wasn't Looking

The eighth-grade girls
in their forest-green Catholic
uniforms and pleated skirts listen
respectfully to the museum guide as she decodes
the mysteries of the statuary looming above
in the rotunda where they stand.   When
the group makes its way towards another room,
schoolgirl penny loafers and sneakers
whispering softly across marbled floor,
one of the girls lingers behind
to gaze up into the distant blank stare
of an alabaster Apollo. Her hand
reaches up to caress the length of his
muscular right calf as both of us
exude a tiny shudder.

Strip Club

Flesh is but part of what we desire,
wandering among fellow husbands and lonely hearts
in search of less hostile company
to simulate *the girlfriend experience*
purchased for forty minutes, time on a meter.

I know the fact that I find
so little offense in how we've spent the past hour
is enough for some to feel seriously offended:
admiring innocuously variable parts of the female anatomy,
the genuine athleticism that enables
a brilliant landing from atop heavily greased pole
wearing seven-inch stiletto platform soles.

But why must there remain
such secrecy? *Omerta!* my friend keeps telling me
sotto voce, like we're planning to rob the till
or kidnap one of the girls.

You can almost taste the fecund smell of this place
as I sip my twenty-dollar beer
and notice my buddy has disappeared
behind a black curtain in the back,
while into his emptied seat slides this buttery soft blonde,
a pastel Renoir nude, fifteen pounds overweight,
her right hand's red nail extensions
digging into my thigh, as she whispers into my ear,
Don't get too comfortable, dear.

Failure

Visionaries find their own way—
legacies born from equal parts talent
and refusal to quit.

Bearing such prodigious gifts
it's easy to overlook the perseverance—
the getting up each morning to paint again,
to drink another cup of bitter coffee
and go back to work.

This was long before any of the work—
pregnant moon star clusters
surfing blue waves across night skies—
auctioned for a hundred million Euros.

What he remembers is less wonderful,
so much failure to overcome:
not lucky in love, not lucky with friends,
not lucky selling the damn paintings.

What he left trumped all:
altars to rolling seas of French countryside
and flaming gardens in midsummer heat,
cypresses and cornfields from a dazzling palette
a brutal tsunami of color paroxysms
that somehow manage to bathe the eye.

In terms of craft, the critics told him
he was a fatally flawed painter
struggling to overcome many technical difficulties:
too decorative, too much caricature,
stick-figure men and women.

Those last two years, bereft of everything,
including half his left ear,
when the frenzy was at its height,
when he nearly disappeared into yellow,

over two hundred paintings racing against
oblivion. How to explain
such commitment rising out of doom:
the will to pursue purple irises
rioting alongside an asylum's cracked wall,
a haloed sower tossing sunflower seeds at barren soil,
the white explosions of peach blossoms
hysterically blooming unattended in some farmer's yard.

Storm at the horizon, crows taking shocked wing,
abdicating wheatfields to brushes and paint,
a last time nature would front its bruised face
to him alone, full circle, recalling that first time
he stretched a canvas and dropped himself down,
those precious few hours in the midst of ecstasy
when beauty reigned.

Scene Observed in Munich's *Neue Pinakothek*

She stands alone,
transfixed by Franz von Stuck's painting

"The Sin," earphones piping museum's interpretation
of snake and femme fatale conjoined
in shadowy blackness.

Is she listening at all, or lost
in her own formulation of what *sin*
looks like?

Her boyfriend,
bored beyond his capacity to concentrate
on such a perfectly blue
Saturday afternoon, tugs at her hips,
nibbles small kisses up and down
her alabaster neck,

insistent to go.

But she is hesitant to leave
the naked dark beauty and her serpentine love
emerging from an interior sea.
She has fallen into their sensuous caress,
they have bound her in their coils,
under their spell, which is, of course,

the whole point of the painting.

She could abandon this silly boy
forever, dump him right here
in this crowded gallery,

even murder him
standing there with restive hands
inside his pockets. The imperious serpent-woman
needs only to command it.

In the Company of Gustav Klimt's Women

For Michael Strauss

I've stumbled into a celestial spa
where all the models are born under the sign Scorpio
and reside in Monaco beach houses.
I am invited into their heavenly-scented space,
although my awkward intrusion is barely noticed
by the nude beauties in their solipsistic adornment
who are acutely more beautiful
because they have just attained orgasm
or are about to.

Clothing is an anathema,
except for those bejeweled and gowned—
living mosaics radiating spectral light.
From beneath a peppermint-flavored sigh,
one of the women says softly to no one in particular:
*Won't you admire the litheness of my alabaster
thighs—how I can roll myself
into this tight little ball without exhaling?*

In this place where weather is indefinitely
postponed, there is nothing to do but daydream
out bedroom windows facing a quiet tree-lined street,
caught in a whisper-soft repose more liquid
than flesh, arms and legs
the weight and texture of ambrosia.
Each of these sloe-eyed, lolling sisters
is accessible, not one is owned by a man,
floating complacently within the ambient ether
of an exclusively feminine universe. A thousand
kohl-rimmed eyes stare out at me unblinking,
like ovulating eggs suspended in a sea of stars.

Hopper's People

For Christopher & Rooster

i.
There is no way to tell
what the middle-aged woman
who sits alone on her bed is thinking
at the moment the pale morning light
enters the room and spills across her nakedness.
Perhaps she is musing on the escape plans
of the businessman reading his evening paper
while his dark-haired wife in half shadow
fumbles absently at the keys on the piano,
already bored with their young marriage,
the brown door on the wall behind them
a simultaneous oasis of possibility
and statement of oppression.

So many curtain-less windows and closed doors
highlighting the clever illusion of paint:
vacant squares and rectangles
that provide no true escape, merely egress
into yet another Hopper interior
that tells a similar story, trapped as we all are
inside our own cubicles of memory
and the compulsion to revisit regret.

People at work fascinated him.
It wasn't the actual work itself
that deserved such attention,
but those performing the work:
some unobtrusive clerk or secretary,
their sexuality cocooned in tight office clothes
that constrain more than they entice.

You would think the world had gone
deaf or that these numbed people,
self-absorbed and lost to each other,

had nothing left to say,
buried beneath the night's sadness inside a diner
or an automat with its stale berry pies
locked behind small glass doors.

A woman wearing a white hat sits at a table
sipping her coffee with one glove on—
the night presses its black face against the window
behind her. A pretty blond usherette
working at a local theater slips a dark sierra
between herself and those watching a film,
then descends into the Technicolor cinema
playing in her own head. And along Main Street
one bright Sunday morning in late summer
only a striped barber pole is awake enough
to make any noise.

ii.
So many dusks have piled up here, identical blurs,
collected like discarded cans of used motor oil.
This is a landscape where you might expect
something startling to occur
at civilization's last outpost before the frontier—
a spaceship to appear overhead,
a blonde wearing red lipstick and driving a red convertible
to pull up seeking directions to Hollywood.
But nothing like that ever happens in this place,
just the hunched shoulders of an innocuous
middle-aged man checking on his three red gas pumps
with their insufferably blank white faces
bolted upright alongside a deserted dirt road
that empties abruptly into pine woods.

Hopper's buildings and shadows
are always more expressive than the people
who reside in space that feels unoccupied.
So, "Gas" is less about the attendant and his gas pumps

than the vista of trees and sky
that exact a quiet whimper
from the man himself—or is it the viewer
who makes this utterance—as both are overwhelmed
by the certain nature of Nature's indifference.

And while the man tries to keep busy,
his station clean and well-lighted, open for business,
the only business to be conducted on this road tonight
concerns an aging man and his thoughts
as darkness descends around him,
and darker still lurks further down the road
at the vanishing point, that bend
where the forest dissolves into green pines
gone shapelessly black.

iii.
Hopper's people wait alone,
even when others inhabit the same room.
We are left to imagine what it is they are
waiting for—the way late autumn sunlight
casts itself on the side of a white house,
evoking a particular emotion that cannot be
easily communicated.

Hopper's people stare blankly
out of open windows and framed doorways.
We are left to imagine what it is they are
looking at: perhaps some tragedy
undergone years ago, but remembered still—
or a premonition about to arrive,
the ineluctable approach of sorrow.

Hopper's people have nowhere to go,
static in sunlight or daydreaming on a train.
We are left to imagine where
they come from and where they are going—

perhaps, if they knew how carefully we have been
observing them, they might pull down the window shade
or go back indoors, shamed by what their clothes
fail to hide.

iv.
When for the last time I touched
the cold alabaster of my horizontal father's
hands and face, both gone hard as marble,
it was like gazing at one of Hopper's
railroad scenes. No train in sight,
it having already passed this junction,
and no future trains on the schedule.
A vacated station house was all that remained
strung with long shadows cast by early
morning light or seamlessly blending
into the sunset's encroaching darkness.
Stretch of empty track leading to nowhere.

Laying Bare the Table

"When correctly viewed, everything is lewd."
—Tom Lehrer

Long before Marxists defined the concept,
the origins of commodity fetishism began
in the Dutch golden age, seventeenth-century
paintings that celebrated the allure of the laden table
in still-life portraits featuring jewels and baubles,
crayfish and lobsters piled high to overflowing,
half blocks of ripened cheeses,
succulent grapes and olives, clams and oysters
glistening on half-shells, hams and rare roast beefs
that promise so much flavor their sheened illusions
still cause us to salivate four hundred years later.

We recognize our own worship at the altar of abundance,
but at the risk of appearing impolite
when must we eschew the proffered plate and knife
to ask: who was provided gristle and gruel
to produce this empire of delectables,
whose dark blood and sweat disrupts
the pristine elegance of this table, this world
where even the burgher himself is displaced
by the dazzling bounty of his larder?

Dora Maar

"I wasn't Picasso's mistress; he was just my master."
—Dora Maar

How then to discern   her place
in between successive wives
for once not just another conquest

             but an accomplice

the only paramour
who could match him in mind
and temperament
                        loved enough
to envision herself   someday
                  inside staid museums
hanging by a thin wire,
                  whole chapters
devoted to their life together
in psychoanalytic biographies.

But they must have both known

             he would leave   her

to wander their Parisian apartment   alone

surrounded by images of   her own
                  tortured face, weeping Magdalenes,
a framed mirror on each wall,

      only her books open behind closed shutters.

But what insight into   that face!
cracking it   to spill out her   howling striations
portrait twisted
                        into immodest revelations.

Did she prove Muse-worthy because

suffering

                                                   was so close to her
                         surfaces,
or was it the painter, his genius

acute to the point where he   foresaw

lost lover, refugee from aborted friendship

anticipated the profundity of her   future sorrow:

                          I want my face back

fragmented   aquamarine   self-effacement
fractured
into   cubist   pieces
until   at last
                                         her every day

caught up with his prophetic pictures,
kohl-lined
                        rivulets
watered by years
                           and tears of salt and birds,
carved eddies
             through viscous paint
the consequence of   a cruel   breaking

her canvas finally
                    done

Vanishing Points

i.
M. Benni appears in my little office
and crosses long nyloned legs
precisely at the knee.
She comes to talk American literature,
but I am thinking Renaissance art,
of Uccello obsessed in his studio
searching for vanishing points,
currents of energy obeying mathematical law—
creation's narrow center at nexus of paint and being.
I am beginning to understand his fascination:
I have recently discovered the vanishing point
of this little office.

ii.
M. Benni's legs are lines of shiny perpendiculars
forever unfolding beneath a chair
at the center of ceiling and floor.
They pull on the solid forms surrounding her;
if not for those tyrants, gravity and repression,
the entire contents of this cubicle—
books, desk, potted palm, professor,
would be sucked down deep
into a vortex of perfection.

iii.
M. Benni insists on knowing why
American writers are drunkneuroticself-
destructivepervertedwomanhaters. I tell her
because American women are not
simpatica, como donni italianne.
M. Benni insists on knowing why
I continue to pronounce *arrivederci*
like an American. I ask her
exactly what does that mean,
but she has already vanished
up from the chair and gone

sweeping the oxygen
out of the room.

Cecil Beaton's Photograph *"Robe en Taffetas de Soie Devant une Peinture de Jackson Pollock"*

Who and what are on display here?
When did great art fuse with a *Vogue* fashion shoot?

Or is Beaton's photograph a statement of Beauty
enhanced by the inclusion of the right accessories?

The model's sculpted white shoulders & blond head
join pink salmon-colored capillaries on bare canvas.

Couture dress, short gloves, & heeled pumps
the exact *noir* of Pollock's permutations. She also brings color:

red lipstick & a pink satin flower attached to her dress,
the painting's rose of a heart.

Parallels give way to projections: paint more animate
than breathing woman, Pollock's lines & arcs send out

electric voltage, leaving the model in static pose.
Art's intimations: twisting parabola and splatter drops

excited by living flesh entering charged space
backdrop for an awkward embrace:

black lightning flashing against white sky. Stare
long enough, there is a moment when the painting

disappears from the room
& the model's mascara streaks into tears.

In Praise of Muses

i
She wondered, *why would anyone want to be a Muse?*
What kind of satisfaction could exist

servicing someone else's flame? I tried to explain
in terms she would most likely

appreciate. It's wielding power,
ultimate control over the production line.

She countered, *birthing is so overrated.*
It's unappreciated toil and sacrifice and pain;

no woman is ever sufficiently warned.
And, in the end, the child always grows up & goes,

leaving you more alone than before.
This is often true, I acknowledged,

both of children and Muses. What matters most
is what they leave behind. Who knew

better than Keats, whose Muse gave birth
in sadness to children of memory and loss,

but children also of exceptional beauty
who continue to dance on the dust of their parents' graves.

ii
Amidst the great bundled-up silences
that are January's burden to bear

you appear
like a surprise delivery of exotic hot house flowers

& my flash-frozen b & w contractions
snap apart in the presence of your global warming.

It is as if I have been granted
sudden entrance into the sequestered garden
of a prolific painter's studio—Matisse will do
nicely—where the painter & I privately tour
his bright canvases one May-splashed morning

absorbing the violets, the reds & yellows & shades of aquamarine
on panels lining the walls.

I know
you have spent hours in front of a mirror today
with your own brushes & colors
in preparation for our meeting.
I see reflected back in
your smoky-lidded eyes & plum mouth,
beauty consigned to a violet pout,

your own pleasure & skill

transforming your face into this pulchritudinous canvas
before me, both of us struck wordless.

I am, in turn, possessed of no better compliment,
no more profound gesture of humbled appreciation,
than the urge to kneel before you

pulling your iridescent face

into intimate contact with mine,
kissing the contours of your delicately ornamented
eyes & cheeks & lips

until both of us are smeared in your paint,

like the happy palette of Matisse himself
who fused new beauty out of everything he destroyed.

Acknowledgements

Many of these poems were originally published elsewhere. Special thanks to the following journals and their editors where they first appeared, sometimes in slightly different form. The majority of the poems in this collection were composed during a sabbatical year made possible by the University of Vermont, for which the author is exceptionally grateful.

Alaska Quarterly Review: "Vanishing Points"
L' Allure des Mots: "When the Museum Guard Wasn't Looking"
Boston Literary Magazine: "She"
Chiron Review: "Language Matters"
Cultural Weekly: "In Praise of Muses"
Earth's Daughters: "Early April Afternoon"
Edgar Allan Poet Journal: "Laying Bare the Table"
Evening Street Press: "Failure"
Foundling Review: "Before This Was My Book"
Gradvia: International Journal of Italian Literature: "Venetian Notes" and "Milan"
Green Mountains Review: "Dracula in Crisis"
Green Writers Press: "Westchester Pastoral"
Harvard Review: "Hopper's People"
Lock Raven Review: "The Essence of Cool" and "Ode to a New Pair of Louboutin Boots"
The Mas Tequila Review: "Paint It Black" (as "Mistress Vader") and "In the Company of Gustav Klimt's Women"
Ocean State Review: "Entropy"
Pamplemousse: "The Brisbane Building" and "In Costco's Parking Lot"
Public Pool: "Strip Club"
Ragazine: "Graduation"
The Salon: "Dora Maar"
Slipstream: "Dialogues Among Lost Tourists" (as "Tourists"), "What Mr. Richel Knew," and "A Short Treatise on Time"
Vermont Literary Review: "My Father's Shoes"
VIA: Voices in Italian Americana: "Tony Soprano Sleeps with the Fishes"

Tony Magistrale is Professor and former chair of the English Department at the University of Vermont where he has taught courses in writing and American literature since 1983 when he returned to the United States after a Fulbright post-doctoral fellowship at the University of Milan, Italy. He has lectured at many universities in North and South America and Western Europe, most recently at Pontificia Catholic University in Santiago, Chile. He obtained a Ph.D at the University of Pittsburgh in 1981

Over the past two decades, Magistrale's twenty-six books and many articles have covered a broad area of interests. He has published on the writing process, international study abroad, and his own poetry. But the majority of his books have centered on defining and tracing Anglo-American Gothicism, from its origins in eighteenth-century romanticism to its contemporary manifestations in popular culture, particularly in the work of Stephen King. He has published three separate interviews with Stephen King, and from 2005-09 Magistrale served as a research assistant to Mr. King. Accordingly, a dozen of his scholarly books and many published journal articles have illuminated the genre's narrative themes, psychological and social contexts, and historical development. He is frequently cited in scholarly books dealing with the interdisciplinary aspects of American horror art, and has been interviewed and/or profiled on PBS television; ABC Radio, Australia; Vermont Public Radio; German Public Radio, ARD; North Carolina Public Radio; Ocean Light Productions, and by the following national and international newspapers and magazines: *The New Yorker, Cinescape, The National Review, The Miami Herald, The Boston Globe, Houston Chronicle, The Baltimore Sun, New York Daily News, The St. Louis Post-Dispatch, The St. Petersburg Times, Movie Geeks United!, Lighthouse Media One* (England), *Oggi* (Italy), *Las Ultimas Noticias* (Chile), and *L'Express* (France).

In 1997, Magistrale received the Kroespsch-Maurice Award for Excellence in Teaching at the University of Vermont. In 2001 he was presented the university's George V. Kidder Outstanding Faculty Award. In 2003 he received the Arts and Sciences Dean's Lecture Award. And in 2010, he was named University Scholar for 2010-11. His newest book is a study of *The Shawshank Redemption*—the film, novella, the history of the Ohio State Reformatory, and their relationship to fan theory—recently published by Palgrave Macmillan.

www.ingramcontent.com/pod-product-compliance
Lightning Source LLC
Chambersburg PA
CBHW021156090426
42740CB00008B/1112